# The Interrogation

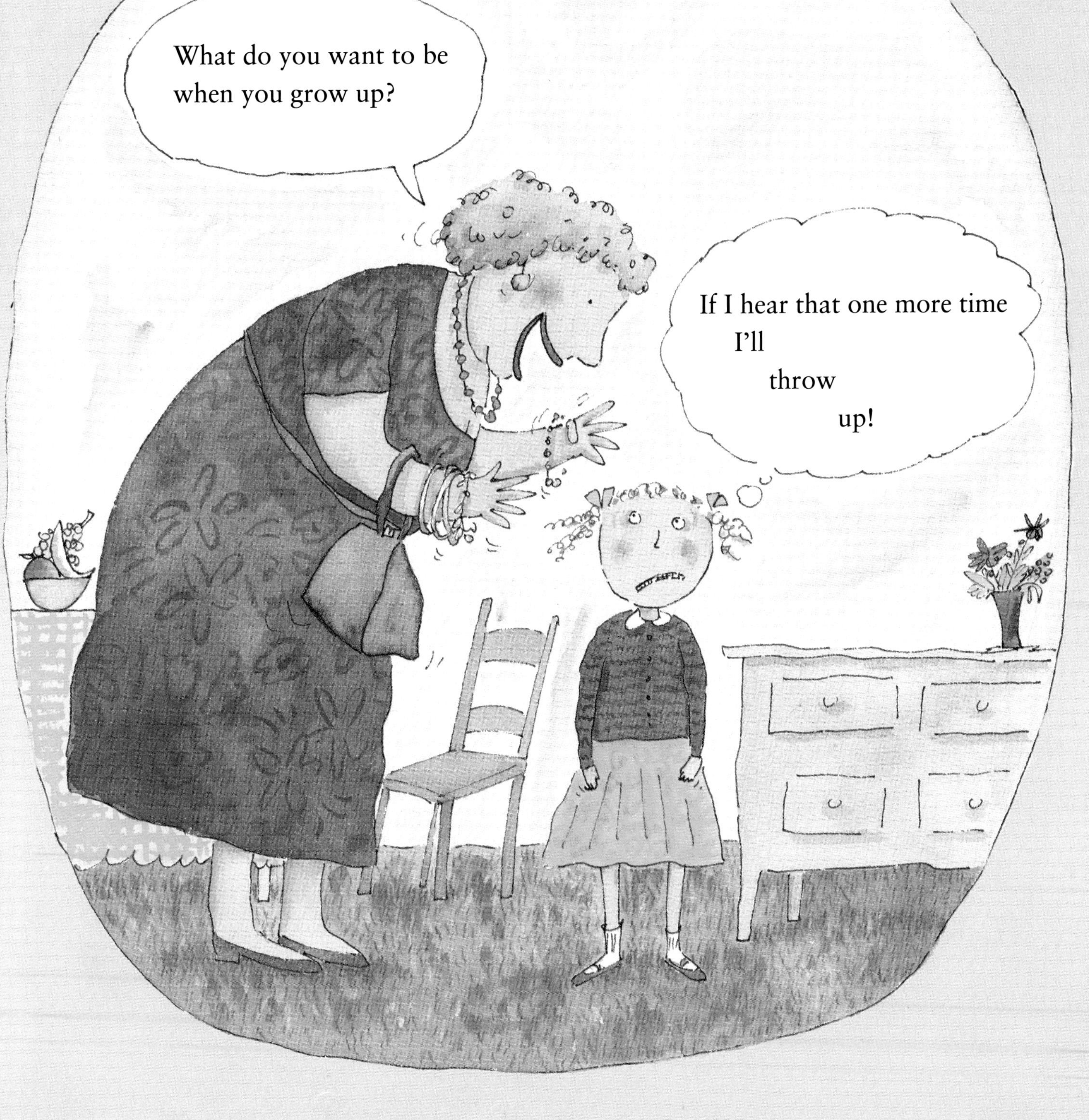

# DANGER: OVERLOAD

"Pick up your clothes,
 wipe your feet,
 set the table,
 it's time to eat.

"Watch the baby,
 close the door,
 throw out the trash,
 and sweep the floor.

"Mail these letters,
 set the clocks,
 put away
 the building blocks.

"Fold the laundry,
 make your bed,
 sort your socks,"
 my mother said.

I swept the baby
with the broom,

threw out the door,
and watched my room.

I washed the trash,
and brushed my socks,
folded the letters,
and mailed the clocks.

No wonder that I got confused—
my mother, though, is not amused.

# Sharing

I used to *hate* sharing.
Now it seems good.
I share my chores—
I think everyone should.

# OUTNUMBERED

We have a big family
and I'm in the middle.
That's why I always
play second fiddle.

I used to call "First!"
but I'd never get it.
I was outnumbered.
Second? Forget it.
Maybe third?
Maybe fourth?
Oh well, I learn fast.
Now to save time
I always call "Last!"

A MELANIE KROUPA BOOK

by
FLORENCE PARRY HEIDE
and
ROXANNE HEIDE PIERCE

illustrated by
Nadine Bernard Westcott

# OH, GROW UP!

## Poems to Help You Survive Parents, Chores, School and Other Afflictions

Orchard Books
New York

To Andy Bauhs,
Longtime neighbor, friend, and family mascot
With love,
The Heide Connection

To Becky
Love, Mom

ORCHARD BOOKS
95 Madison Avenue
New York, NY  10016

Manufactured in the United States of America
Printed by Barton Press, Inc.
Bound by Horowitz / Rae
Book design by Sylvia Frezzolini Severance

10  9  8  7  6  5  4  3  2

The text of this book is set in 13.5 point Sabon.
The illustrations are done with black ink line and watercolors.

Library of Congress Cataloging-in-Publication Data

Heide, Florence Parry.
    Oh, grow up! : poems to help you survive parents, chores,
school, and other afflictions / by Florence Parry Heide and
Roxanne Heide Pierce ; illustrated by Nadine Bernard Westcott.
      p.  cm.
    "A Melanie Kroupa book."
Summary: A collection of poems about surviving daily life
presented from a child's point of view.
      ISBN 0-531-09471-5.  —  ISBN 0-531-08771-9 (lib. bdg.)
      1. Life skills — Juvenile poetry. 2. Children's poetry, American.
[1. American poetry — Collections.]  I. Pierce, Roxanne Heide.
II. Westcott, Nadine Bernard, ill.  III. Title.
PS3558.E42703  1996
811'.54 — dc20                              95-23177

# MY HALF

I share a room
with brother Bob.
We share a bunk bed, too.
Half the room belongs to me,
and half to you-know-who.
Of course it's fair to share a room,
but yet I have the feeling
that since I'm on the upper bunk
my half's just on the ceiling.

# SCARING MY SISTER

My sister wasn't scared a bit
when I said there was a bear
with bloody claws and dripping fangs
coming up the stair.

She wasn't even worried
that gorillas roamed the house,
or that a vicious vampire bat
just ate her brand-new blouse.

She never even blinked an eye
when she heard about the snakes
that writhed around her bedpost
leaving mucous in their wakes.

But she really paid attention
when I said her boyfriend called
and said he'd found another girl —
Oh, ouch!
My hair!
I'm bald!

# BRACES

My braces have been on for years.
They're coming off next week.
I can hardly wait to see
if there are teeth beneath.

## Sitting for Susie

Making lunch for Susie
is such an awful bore.
Everything I try to fix
just makes her whine some more.

The hot dog's never hot enough,
the bun tastes like a stick,
the Jell-O is too wiggly,
the milk looks much too thick.

The carrot sticks are short and hard,
she wanted chips instead,
the pickles are too small and thin,
the ketchup is too red.

The Popsicle is too ice-cold,
she whined and sulked and cried.
I put it in the microwave—
she's *still* not satisfied.

# HAND-ME-DOWNS

My older sister Jill wears plaid:
plaid shirts, plaid skirts, plaid bows.
I hate, despise, detest the stuff
as everybody knows.
But Mom and Dad still make me wear
all her outgrown clothes.

I prefer a different style
plain as plain can be.
My sister says she'd give up clothes
if she had taste like me.

Something different's happening now:
I'm growing pretty fast.
Soon she'll have to wear *my* clothes
and I'll wear plain at last.

# Taking Turns

I can't get into the bathroom.
My sister's in there still.
I wonder when she'll come back out,
or if she ever will.

Taking a bath
curling her hair
washing her fancy underwear
hanging her pantyhose everywhere—
I never knew
so many things
could be done in there—
tweezing her eyebrows
doing her face
painting her toenails
running in place.

I'm finally in the bathroom.
I got in yesterday.
I've brought my sleeping bag and stuff—
oh yes, I'm here to stay.

My sister's pounding on the door.
I hear her scream and shout.
I'll read this stack of comic books—
then *maybe* I'll come out.

# The Pet

They said I couldn't have a dog—
my dad is strict, my mom is stricter—
so I didn't get a dog:
I got a boa constrictor.

I call him Victor.

Warning
Do Not Enter
Stop
Wrong Way
Beware
Danger
Do Not Trespass
Caution
Don't You Dare

I taped the signs onto the door—
I thought that's all I'd need.

My brother came in anyway—
He hasn't learned to read.

# MONSTER of SLOB

My room's a mess, an awful mess.
What all is here, I just can't guess.
Mildewed towels and muddy shoes,
Paints and paste I never use.
Banana peels and wads of gum,
A rusty old aquarium.
Dirty socks and Tuesday's snack,
A suitcase that I should unpack.
No place to stand, no place to sit—
Say—isn't that pile shifting a bit?
Isn't it moving closer to me?
Is that a pair of eyes I see?
Is that an arm that's reaching out?
Is that a claw? Is that a snout?
I see its face, and now I see
it's really coming after me.
I should have listened when Mom said
to clean my room and make my bed.
My mess has changed, I don't know how.
It's turned into a monster now.

I march that monster out the door
and follow it outside.
I watch it as it lumbers off. . . .
It turns to wave good-bye.

The mess is gone.
My room is clean.
My parents will be glad.
But me, I really miss my mess—
the best I've ever had.

If I start now
and work real fast,
I can get it done:
I'll start a new mess right away—
a bigger, better one!

# TAKING OUT THE GARBAGE

It's my turn to take out the garbage.
I really hate doing this chore.
And—whoops! there go some eggshells
and—whoops! there slip some more.
There slide some fish bones and diapers—
I'm making a long, slimy trail
down to the end of the driveway—
I'm careful not to inhale.
My parents will notice my efforts.
They'll be sad for a moment and then—
I know I never will have to
take out the garbage again.

## DOUBLES

"I need my allowance, Mom,"
 I say.
"I really need it bad!"
"All right," says Mom, "then here it is."
And now I'll go ask Dad.

## GROUNDED

I'm grounded.
I said a bad word and I'm grounded.
I just wanted to hear how it sounded.
It sounded great,
so I said it again
and taught it to my brother.
We agreed it was a *good* bad word—
but it didn't sound good to my mother!

# Advice

Parents like to give advice.
They'll say it once,
they'll say it twice,
a thousand times,
to be precise:
Should and Shouldn't
Must and Daren't—
how *do* you learn
to be a parent?

There must be very special schools
that teach the parents all the rules,
so they can give their kids advice
about what's naughty and what's nice.

My parents got good grades, I bet—
probably the best ones yet—
A's in NO's and A's in DON'Ts
A *pluses* in Oh-no-you-won'ts.
(They weren't perfect all the way—
they got an F in Yes-you-may.)

I only have one life to live—
my parents want to live it.
If only *I* could give advice,
I'd tell them
      just don't give it!

# Dinner at a Fancy Restaurant

Staring at the menu,
this is what I see:
a list of all my choices
staring back at me.

Liver and Calves Brains
Veal Scallopini
Oysters Pierre
Clam Sauce Linguine

Everyone has ordered now—
all eyes are glued on me.
I scan the menu one more time
a little desperately.

I hear my father
clear his throat.
I hear the waiter mutter,
"And you, monsieur,
what weel eet be?"

"I weesh La Peanut Butter."

# DAD'S NIGHT TO COOK

Leftover chili,
leftover stew,
something that looks
like leftover glue,
leftover omelet,
dried-up chicken pies,
leftover tuna-and-noodle-surprise,
leftover pizza,
leftover ham,
leftover waffles,
and barbequed lamb.

Our father really hates to cook—
he'll use up what we've got.
He'll just throw every single thing
in one enormous pot.
He'll heat it up
and then we'll have
a crazy mixed-up brew,
a bubbling and repulsive mess. . . .
He calls it Gourmet Stew.

# Query

Could anything be drearier
than the food in the school cafeteria?

## My Principal Objection

The principal reason I hate school
is our principal, Mr. Peter P. Pool.
He's always on my case a lot,
whether I've done wrong or not.

It's not that I hate school this spring—
I guess it's the *principal* of the thing.

## HISTORY

I just don't feel like going to school.
There's a test today—
dates and names and distant places,
things to know, like "Where's Bombay?"

I'm not prepared—I just won't go.
No, history's not for me.

But Mom just said
if I don't go
then *I'll* be history.

# THE BLACKBOARD BULLY

I stand at the blackboard and groan when I see
the meanest big bully, Slimy McGee,
that dough-faced, pudding-faced, weasel-faced creep
who's made my days dreadful and ruined my sleep.
He pinches my arm and stomps on my toes,
he pushes me down and spits on my clothes,
he erases my math and the rest of my work,
he steals all my answers and then he'll just smirk,
he erases my name and all of my spelling
and then he just sneers, "I know you're not telling."
I wouldn't *dare* tell. But what can I do?
How can I lose him?  I haven't a clue.

Wait!
Here's an idea!
I turn and I face him,
I take a deep breath . . .

and then I erase him!

## What? No School Today?

There won't be school, I'm sure of it.
It snowed too much last night.
Just look at it! There's just no way!
There can't be school now, right?
I'll play all day! I love today!
I feel so wide awake!
I'll even shovel—I've got time
to get rid of every flake.

Oh, yipeeeeee!

What? What did you say?
There's school today? Who said?
We have to go? With all this snow?
I'm going back to bed!

# SCARY STORIES

Ellen slept over again last night
and when we were ready for bed,
she told scary stories
trying to scare me . . .
but she scared herself instead.

# The Guest

My cousin's name is Genevieve. . . .
I wish she'd leave.

# PROBLEM

"Make your bed,"
  my mother said.
"I'll make it in a minute!"
  I don't know how
  to make it now
  because I'm still tucked in it!

7

DISCARD